SPEED!
PLANES

Jenifer Corr Morse

BLACKBIRCH PRESS, INC.

WOODBRIDGE, CONNECTICUT

To Alexander Samuel Morse
May you always find reading to be one of life's greatest adventures.
–JCM

Published by Blackbirch Press, Inc.
260 Amity Road
Woodbridge, CT 06525
Web site: www.blackbirch.com
e-mail: staff@blackbirch.com

© 2001 Blackbirch Press, Inc.
First Edition

Printed in Belgium

10 9 8 7 6 5 4 3 2 1

Photo Credits
Cover, back cover (top), pages 1, 4-7, 15, 18-23: Corel Corporation; back cover (bottom): PhotoDisc; page 8: PhotoDisc; pages 9-11: courtesy of Lockheed Martin; page 13: NASA; page 14: US Navy/DOD/Time, Inc.; page 16: John Farmer; Cordaiy Photo Library Ltd/CORBIS.

Library of Congress Cataloging-in-Publication Data
Morse, Jenifer Corr.
    Planes / By Jenifer Morse.
    p. cm. — (Speed!)
    Includes index.
    ISBN 1-56711-466-0
    1. Airplanes—Juvenile literature. [1. Airplanes.] I Title. II. Speed! (Woodbridge, Conn.)

TL547 .M675 2001
629.133'34—dc21   00-011895

Contents

AV-8B Harrier

Can hover, take off, and land vertically

The AV-8B Harrier is a truly amazing fighter jet. It is known as a short-takeoff/vertical landing craft (STOVL). It is one of only a few fighter attack aircraft that can take off and land vertically. That means the AV-8B Harrier can lift off or land by going directly up or down—most of the time there's no runway needed! In fact, during Desert Storm, an AV-8B squadron was able to take off from, and land on, a ship that was used to launch helicopters!

The Harrier is also one of the only jets in the world that can hover—holding its place in the air without moving.

Cruising along at sea level, this Marine Corps plane can reach speeds of 660 miles (1,062 km) per hour. At higher altitudes, its speed is reduced to almost 600 miles (965 km) per hour. A powerful Rolls-Royce F402-RR-408 turbofan engine gives the AV-8B its speed and ability. The Harrier is designed for only one pilot.

Fast Fact

* Length: 46.4 ft (14.1 m)
* Wingspan: 30.4 ft (9.2 m)

The AV-8Bs are used for many different missions. Sometimes they escort military helicopters into dangerous territory. Other times, AV-8Bs engage in air combat, or attack enemy ground equipment.

At sea level, the Harrier can fly at 660 miles (1,062 km) per hour.

There are several types of weapons that can be carried on board the AV-8B. One of the more advanced weapons delivery systems includes the Angle Rate Bombing System (ARBS). This has laser and television target seekers and trackers. The Harrier can also carry AIM-9 Sidewinder missiles, Harpoon anti-ship missiles, and GBU-10 laser-guided bombs. The plane's highly advanced radar allows it to perform well in any weather conditions and at night.

F-16 Fighting Falcon

Incredible control at high speeds, and the best combat radius of any fighter

The F-16 Fighting Falcon is one of the most valuable planes used by the U.S. Air Force. Its incredible control and long combat radius (distance it can fly to a destination, engage in combat, and return home) are far better than any aircraft it may face in battle. Zipping along at 1,500 miles (2,414 km) per hour, the Falcon is very hard to catch. The aircraft can also fly in any weather conditions. It can deliver weapons without seeing its target and it can spot low flying planes with its super-advanced radar.

The Falcon is able to reach speeds of 1,500 miles (2,414 km) per hour.

F-16Cs are flown by only one pilot, but F-16Ds have two.

The F-16C is flown by one pilot, but the F-16D has a two-person crew. These fighters are used mostly for air-to-air combat. They are also used to attack Scud missile sites, airfields, military production sites, and other important enemy targets.

These sleek fighting machines cost about $20 million per plane. Currently in the United States, there are 444 F-16s in active force. An additional 305 planes are in the Air National Guard, and 60 are in reserve. Fighting Falcons are also used in many other countries, including Israel, Egypt, Belgium, and Norway.

●≡*Fast* ≡*Fact* ●

★ Length: 49.5 ft   (14.8 m)
★ Wingspan: 32.6 ft   (9.8 m)
★ Height: 16 ft   (4.8 m)

The Fighting Falcon can withstand nine times the force of gravity—more than any other fighter plane. It is armed with one 20-millimeter 6-barrel cannon that can fire 500 rounds. It can also carry up to six air-to-air or air-to-surface missiles.

Lockheed SR-71

The "Blackbird" is the fastest jet in the world.

The Lockheed SR-71 is the fastest jet in the world. It has reached an awesome top speed of 2,193.2 miles (3,529 km) per hour. That's three times the speed of sound! At that rate, the aircraft could fly from New York to California in a little more than 80 minutes! The SR-71 can fly at top speed for an hour before it needs to refuel (which it can do on the ground or in the air).

When the SR-71 flies at high speeds, the air friction heats the edges of the plane to almost 800°F (426° C). To help reduce the temperature, the aircraft is built around a titanium frame. It is also painted with heat-reflecting black paint. This paint gives the plane the nickname "Blackbird."

The Blackbird weighs more than 70 tons.

The Blackbird can fly at a top speed of 2,193 miles (3,529 km) per hour.

Of all the world's jet-powered aircraft, the SR-71 is the one aircraft that can reach the highest altitude. This plane is able to soar up to 88,000 feet (26,822 m) above the ground. Because the pressure is very low at that altitude, pilots must wear special pressurized suits.

The Blackbird has a gross weight of 140,000 pounds (63,504 kg) and is powered by 2 Pratt and Whitney high-bypass turbojets. Together, these engines produce about 65,000 pounds (29,484 kg) of thrust.

● ≡*Fast* ≡*Fact* ●

★ Length: 107.5 ft (33 m)
★ Wingspan: 55.5 ft   (17 m)
★ Height: 18.6 ft   (5.6 m)

The U.S. Air Force first used these supersonic planes in 1964. Today, the majority of the SR-71s have been retired. NASA, however, has used the aircraft to carry out high-altitude research.

Raptors can cruise at 1.5 times the speed of sound.

● Fast Fact ●

★Length: 62 ft   (19 m)
★Wingspan: 44 ft   (13.4 m)

Each F22 aircraft can carry six radar-guided AIM-120C advanced medium-range air-to-air missiles in its main cargo area. In each of its two side bays, there is room for a heat-seeking AIM-9 Sidewinder short-range missile. The F22 also has a gun system capable of firing ammunition at a rate of 100 rounds per second.

F22 Raptor

One of the world's most advanced fighter planes

The Raptor is one of the most technologically advanced U.S. fighter planes in existence. It is known for its stealth, speed, and control. On enemy radar, the Raptor looks like it's about the same size as a bumblebee! This is because it reflects radar in a special way. The F22's weapons are also located inside the plane so they do not create additional surface features that would be easily picked up by enemy radar.

By carrying its weapons internally, the F22 is also more aerodynamic. This means that air flows most easily over the plane as it flies. The smooth flow of air means less wind resistance to slow the machine down. The F22 is capable of flying at Mach 1.5 (1.5 times the speed of sound). Two F119-PW-100 engines power it, each delivering 35,000 pounds (15,876 kg) of thrust.

The Raptor was developed in the late 1990s at a cost of about $13 billion. It has undergone the most sophisticated testing of any U.S. combat aircraft. The F22 program will have a total of 333 planes, each costing approximately $84 million.

Raptors are highly aerodynamic.

North American X-15

These rocket-propelled planes traveled to the outer edge of the atmosphere and reached Mach 6.

During their short service time between 1959 and 1968, the North American X-15s set several incredible flying records. These rocket-propelled planes were the first fixed-wing aircraft to reach Mach 6—a speed of 4,534 miles (7,297 km) per hour! The X-15, which was built to learn more about high-speed flight, was carried 40,000 feet (12,000 m) into the air under the wing of a Boeing B-52 bomber. It was then detached, and fired up its rockets to create its own thrust.

On its own, one X-15 was actually able to reach an altitude of 354,000 feet (107,899 m). That means the plane was 67 miles (107.8 km) above Earth—the outer edge of our planet's atmosphere!

Two of the X-15's design features were key in allowing the plane to perform so well. First, the plane's wedge-shaped tail helped to stabilize the aircraft while it flew at such high speeds. The downward-slanting wings, along with the upper and lower fins, also helped keep the plane stabilized during its steep climbs at high altitudes.

● Fast Fact ●

- ★ Length: 51 ft   (15.5 m)
- ★ Wingspan: 13 ft   (4 m)
- ★ Height: 22 ft   (6.7 m)

Most of the experiments and research carried out on the X-15 flights was used to develop and improve the Space Shuttle. One of the last surviving X-15s can be seen at the National Air and Space Museum in Washington, D.C.

The X-15 is the only plane ever to reach Mach 6.

The X-15 cockpit.

Rocket thrusters on the rear gave the X-15 its incredible speed and power.

MiG-25

The Russian-built "Foxbat" is the world's fastest combat jet.

The MiG-25 can reach a top speed of 1,865 miles (3,000 km) per hour.

The Russian MiG-25 is the world's fastest combat jet. At high altitudes, this aircraft can reach speeds up to 1,865 miles (3,000 km) per hour. At sea level, the speed drops to 745 miles (1,200 km) per hour. Nicknamed "Foxbat" by NATO forces, the MiG-25 is powered by two R-15B-300 single shaft turbojets capable of producing 49,400 pounds (10,890 kg) of thrust.

The MiG-31 Foxhound is also fast—it can travel at Mach 2.8.

Even though this plane is fast, its bulky frame prevents it from engaging in close air-to-air combat. The main purpose of the MiG-25 is to intercept speedy enemy aircraft. It carries 4 R-40 air-to-air missiles that have a range from 1 to 37 miles (2 to 60 km). Equipped with powerful, long-range radar, the Foxbat is also capable of launching guided missiles at ground targets. Its anti-radar Kh-58 missiles can also wipe out enemy radar.

This large interceptor aircraft has an empty weight of 44,092 pounds (19,986 kg). The MiG-25 is flown by one pilot.

Fast Fact

- ★ Length: 78 ft   (23.8 m)
- ★ Wingspan: 46 ft   (14 m)
- ★ Height: 20 ft   (6.1 m)

Designed between 1958 and 1962, the Foxbat entered service in 1968. Several European and Middle Eastern countries, including Russia, Ukraine, Iraq, Iran, and Syria currently use this aircraft.

Super Lynx Helicopter

Able to fly up to 250 miles (402 km) per hour, this is the world's fastest helicopter.

Two Rolls-Royce engines power the Super Lynx Helicopter.

The Super Lynx is the fastest helicopter in the world. It is capable of flying 250 miles (402 km) per hour, which is very unusual for a typically slow-moving vehicle. Two Rolls-Royce Gem 42-1 turboshaft engines power the Super Lynx. It has a 184-cubic-foot (5.2-cu-m) cabin that can hold 2 crewmembers and 9 troops.

Approximately 200 Lynx helicopters are in service with 11 navies around the world. The aircraft are very useful

Fast Fact

★ Length: 50 ft   (15.2 m)
★ Height: 12 ft   (3.6 m)

The design of the Lynx and its landing gear allow it to operate from small ships at sea. It has a harpoon locking system that secures the aircraft to the deck after landing. The wheels can still be moved, however, which allows the Lynx to turn into the wind while it is still anchored to the deck. This prevents the ship from having to change course.

because they can perform several different operations. They are able to bomb land targets, as well as submarines. These helicopters are super fast, but they also have the ability to hover above land and water. Lynx are frequently used in search and rescue missions. Lynx helicopters are also used to move supplies and machinery to, from, and between ships. A hook located on the underside of the aircraft can hold up to 3,000 pounds (1,360 kg) of cargo.

Concorde

The only passenger jet able to fly faster than the speed of sound

The Concorde is the only supersonic (faster than the speed of sound) passenger aircraft. Once it reaches its cruising altitude of 55,000 feet (16,764 m), the Concorde flies at 1,336 miles (2,150 km) per hour. That's twice the speed of sound! The beginning and end of the flight are also quick—the plane takes off at a speed of 250 miles (402 km) per hour and lands at 187 miles (300 km) an hour.

The plane uses 4 Rolls-Royce/SNECMA Olympus 593 engines, each producing a thrust of 38,000 pounds (17,236 kg). These powerful engines also make the Concorde the loudest passenger plane ever built. The vehicle can carry 100 passengers and 1,300 pounds (454 kg) of cargo. Because of the $9,000-a-seat price tag, however, celebrities and wealthy business people are often the only passengers.

Fast Fact

★ Length: 204 ft   (62.1 m)
★ Wingspan: 83.8 ft   (25.5 m)

The Concorde carries approximately 31,500 gallons (119,236 l) of fuel per flight, but only burns about 27,000 gallons (102,203 l). The remaining fuel is used to balance the plane as it flies along at Mach 2.

The Concorde was first introduced in 1976. Today British Airways has seven of the aircraft in service, and Air France has five. They mainly offer flights between New York and London. Because the flights only take about 3.5 hours, and the Concorde crosses 5 time zones, sometimes passengers can actually arrive before they leave! For example, if a plane leaves London at 5:00 p.m., it will arrive in New York at 3:30 p.m. because of the 5-hour time difference.

Concordes carry passengers at twice the speed of sound.

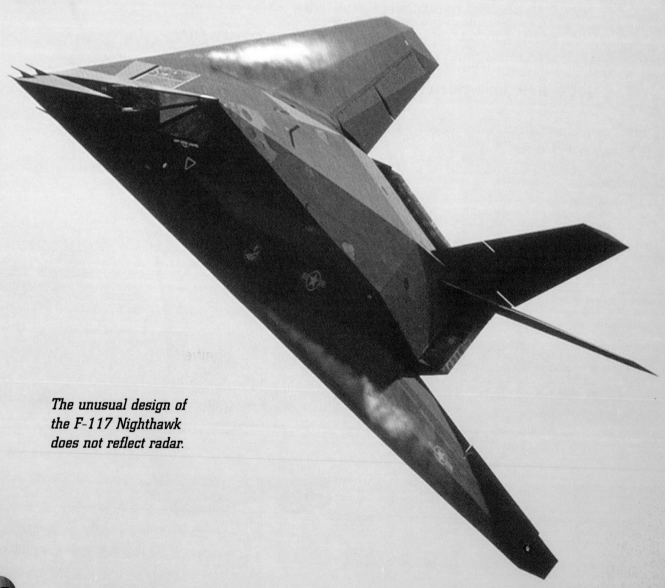

The unusual design of the F-117 Nighthawk does not reflect radar.

F-117 Nighthawk

Using its advanced radar-deflecting technology, this bomber is able to fly through enemy skies undetected.

The F-117 Nighthawk is truly a "stealth bomber." Its clever design makes it virtually undetectable by enemy radar. The unusual shape of the plane is made from many different angles that make it invisible to reflect monitoring radar. Its weapons are stored inside, which means they also go undetected. The F-117's exhaust is cooled and filtered through small holes in the aircraft. That means the hot exhaust is not picked up by heat-seeking radar. And, there is a dark, radar-absorbing material (RAM) that coats the entire aircraft. Even the name is meant to cause confusion. The "F" in F-117 stands for "fighter," but the plane is really a light bomber.

The F-117 was built as a top-secret bomber for the U.S. Air Force and was first flown in 1982. The bombs carried aboard the aircraft can accurately guide themselves to their targets. In fact, during the Gulf War in 1991, an F-117 managed to destroy a Scud missile facility by sending a laser-guided bomb into the building's air duct.

Fast Fact

* Length: 66 ft (20 m)
* Wingspan: 43 ft (13 m)

The Nighthawk can fly into areas without being detected, so it does not have to fly at supersonic speeds to escape danger. Flown by a single pilot, the top speed of an F-117 Nighthawk is 700 miles (1,126 km) per hour.

TU-95 Bear

The fastest propeller-driven plane in history

The TU-95 Bear was developed by Russia in the early 1950s. It is the only bomber plane used in war that had a turboprop engine. In fact, this aircraft used four turboprop engines that each controlled two sets of propellers. One set of propellers turned clockwise, the other set turned counterclockwise. This type of engine allowed the TU-95 to cruise over long distances at around 270 miles (434 km) per hour. It was, however, able to reach a top speed of 575 miles (925 km) per hour, which makes it the fastest propeller-driven aircraft in history. Since it was able to fly for long distances, this bomber was also used as a patrol plane over large bodies of water.

With a maximum height of 44,000 feet (13,411 m), the TU-95 was able to fly up to 7,500 miles (12,069 km) while carrying up to 19,840 pounds (9,000 kg) of bombs. If the range was shortened, the bombers were able to carry more weapons. During longer missions, the plane was able to refuel in the air. Each aircraft also had six radar-controlled AM-23 guns to defend itself from enemy attack.

The Russian TU-95 Bear could reach a top speed of 575 miles (925 km) per hour.

Fast Fact

★ Length: 160 ft   (49 m)
★ Wingspan: 167 ft   (51 m)

This aircraft, developed in the 1950s, carried a crew of seven. Special radar located under the nose of the aircraft helped the TU-95 to monitor enemy planes and navigate its course.

Glossary

altitude: the height of something above the ground
friction: rubbing
intercept: to stop the movement of something
resistance: a force that goes against the motion of an object
squadron: a group of ships, cavalry troops, or other military units
thrust: the forward force produced by the engine of a jet or rocket

For More Information

Books

Collins, Jonathan. *Modern Commercial Aircraft.* New York, NY: Chelsea House, 1997.

Maynard, Chris. *Aircraft: The Need For Speed.* Minneapolis, MN: Lerner Publications, 1999.

Schleifer, Jay. *Fighter Planes.* Danbury, CT: Children's Press, 1998.

Web Site

National Air and Space Museum
Learn about the history of aviation—**www.nasm.edu**

Index